THE LAW OF THE LAND
Debating National Land Use
Legislation 1970-75

by

Noreen Lyday

THE URBAN INSTITUTE is a nonprofit research organization established in 1968 to study problems of the nation's urban communities. Independent and nonpartisan, the Institute responds to current needs for disinterested analyses and basic information and attempts to facilitate the application of this knowledge. As a part of this effort, it cooperates with federal agencies, states, cities, associations of public officials, and other organizations committed to the public interest.

The Institute's research findings and a broad range of interpretive viewpoints are published as an educational service. The research and studies forming the basis for this publication were supported by a grant from the Ford Foundation. The work was undertaken in The Urban Institute's Land Use Center.

The interpretations or conclusions are those of the author and should not be attributed to The Urban Institute, its trustees, the Ford Foundation, or other organizations that support its research.

Contents

Foreword

The debate over national land use legislation which began in 1970 and continued for more than five years, was characterized by much confusion over ends and means. At the heart of the debate were basic questions about what kind of growth we should have, where it should be located and the proper roles of government and the private sector in making these decisions. Both Congress and the President took an active lead in attempting to resolve these issues.

Legislation was first introduced by powerful Democrats in the Ninety-First Congress. The Nixon Administration also supported land use legislation though in a somewhat different form. Both proposals called for strengthening the hand of state governments to deal with problems of growth—one through state planning and the other by shifting some regulatory authority from local to state government. Ultimately the two approaches were combined into one piece of legislation. The bill seemed to enjoy widespread if less than enthusiastic support during the early 1970s but ultimately it was defeated in an emotionally charged atmosphere amid charges and counter-charges about the bill's intent and its likely effects.

This report traces the origins of the bills and the response of interest groups who played a major role in either support or opposition. It attempts to uncover some of the assumptions that underlay the various bills, to show how they were shaped by the pressure of events and ideologies, and to analyze the legislation's defeat. The paper reveals that while consensus could be reached on the general proposition that growth should, somehow, be controlled, that consensus quickly disappeared when the implications of control were probed. Positions on national land use policy were governed largely by quite different, but equally plausible assumptions about who would win and lose should a bill be enacted. In part, this was a reflection of our limited understanding of the forces that shape and determine growth. It was also the result of not having a clear and suitably limited concept of the role of government in controlling growth. On the positive side, the debate over national land use policy raised the issue as a subject of serious research and discussion. Also, as a paper in this series by Nelson Rosenbaum, *Land Use and the Legislatures,* argues, it played an important role in stimulating many states to assume greater responsibility for land use.

While the author questions whether passage of the type of land use legislation debated over the last five years would have made any real difference in the problems it was addressed to, the history of the debate and the continuing concern over how we grow suggests that having failed in one attempt, the search should not be abandoned.

This is the third in a continuing series of reports on current issues in land use, prepared under the direction of Worth Bateman of The Urban Institute's Land Use Center.

William Gorham
President
September 1976   The Urban Institute

Acknowledgments

Worth Bateman, Director of the Institute's Land Use Center, originally proposed this analysis of the recent history of national land use legislation. His encouragement and support throughout the project has been invaluable. Without the help of the many people interviewed in the course of this project, including major participants in the legislative debate, this study would not have been possible. Nelson Rosenbaum, George Peterson, and Grace Dawson of the Land Use Center all provided helpful comments and criticisms on earlier drafts.

I. Introduction: The Time Seemed Ripe

In the early 1970's the stage seemed to be set for passage of a national land use policy bill. On January 1, 1970 President Nixon signed the National Environmental Policy Act (NEPA), the first legislation to become law in the new decade. The 70's promised to be, the President said, the "decade of the environment."

Four weeks later, Senator Henry M. Jackson, Chairman of the Senate Interior Committee and the author of NEPA, introduced the first National Land Use Policy Bill, a bill which he called "the next logical step (to NEPA) in our national effort to provide a quality life in a quality environment. . . ." Jackson's bill would have provided money to develop state land use plans. Plans drawn up by each state would identify where to put projects like airports, powerplants, housing developments and parks. In Jackson's view, this was the way to avoid—or at least reduce—the increasingly bitter clashes between the environmentalists and the developers; the way to assure economic growth and, at the same time, protect the environment.

Throughout 1970 the Senator urged the Administration either to support his bill or develop one of its own. The Administration took the latter tack early in 1971. The Administration's bill, drawn up at the new Council on Environmental Quality, proposed that some of the land use regulatory authority traditionally exercised by local governments be shifted to the states. It was, in some ways, a more modest bill than Jackson's. The Administration proposed that states assume authority to regulate what were called "critical areas and uses." Critical areas and uses were never precisely defined but were roughly specified as (1) areas where development might damage important historic, cultural, or aesthetic values, or natural systems; (2) key facilities or public works like airports, highway interchanges that tend to induce development; (3) large-scale private development like major subdivisions which, because of their size, might create pollution or congestion in neighboring jurisdictions and (4) developments and land uses of "regional benefit." The state's authority in the latter case was to be limited to overriding local land use regulations that were restrictive or exclusionary. The Administration viewed its proposal as "institutional reform" with the rationale that states should assume authority to control private development where the impacts were regional rather than purely local.

In June of 1972 the Administration bill and the earlier Jackson bill were combined into a single piece of legislation. It was this combined planning and regulatory reform measure that was debated in the Congress for the next three years. During most of this time the bill was touted as "major environmental legislation" by both the Administration and the bill's sponsors

1

and supporters in the Congress. The bill had powerful support on the Hill. Senator Jackson was the chief Senate sponsor and in the House, the bill became priority legislation when Congressman Morris Udall of Arizona succeeded to the Chairmanship of the House Interior Committee's Subcommittee on the Environment in 1973.

The bill passed the Senate twice, first in 1972 and again in 1973. Both times it passed with a solid majority. In January 1974 the President called passage of the bill a "high priority" of his Administration and "the most pressing environmental issue before the nation." At the same time, Congressman Udall was confidently predicting that the bill would pass within a few months. Then, in February 1974, the House Rules Committee by a vote of 9-4 refused to order the bill reported to the House floor for a vote. The bill, which just a few months earlier had seemed to enjoy widespread and powerful support, was in deep trouble in the House. Ultimately, the Rules Committee reconsidered and the bill was ordered out so that Congress could vote on the proposed legislation. On June 12, 1974, the bill was defeated (on a procedural vote). The proponents charged "impeachment politics." In fact, there was massive confusion about the bill's intent and concern about its effect on private property rights and the traditional institutional framework for making land use decisions.

Critics charged that "the bill would give the Secretary of the Interior the right to control every piece of land in the nation," that it was a "Federal zoning bill." More damaging was the charge that the bill's implicit, if not explicit purpose was to bribe the states to use their police power to prevent development on privately owned land for purposes that, in the opponents' view, were anti-growth, aesthetic and elitist.

The bill's advocates, on the other hand, maintained that the bill was a policy-neutral, states-rights bill which left it to the states to determine what lands should be protected. They argued that the legislation would have no effect on Constitutional protections afforded private property rights. The limits to the police power, the point at which regulation so restricts a property owner's rights that compensation is required, were not to be resolved in the national legislation but in each of the separate states. The bill's purpose, they explained, was to help the states plan and manage their land for "wise and balanced use." It was this vagueness about ends and suspicion about intent, at a time when earlier enthusiasm for "environmental initiatives" had cooled, that allowed opponents to raise the charges that ultimately led to the bill's defeat.

The issues which the land use bill raised are important. They are, ultimately, questions about growth and development; how much, what kind, where, who shall decide, and how can these decisions be made equitably.

Unfortunately, the land use bill and the debate did little to illuminate these issues. The debate over the "takings" issue, while important, overwhelmed all other issues. In the heat of debate on this extremely emotional issue, public decisions became equated with the use of the police power and the debate over the police power revealed that the advocates of extending this power to protect "critical environmental areas" had not made their case.

It is not the purpose of this paper to analyze the many complex issues implicit in the land use debate. Rather, this is the story of how the bill got on the national agenda and of its journey through the legislative process; the story of how the process worked to produce a bill which generated much confusion with respect to both legislative intent and effect. What did its authors hope to achieve? What evidence did they have to suppose that a land use bill would favorably alter present land use patterns and decision-making processes? Who supported the bill, who opposed it and why? What were the assumptions that underlay the bill—assumptions about the problem, its causes, about the real change that would flow from reform? If the critics' charges seemed excessive, what about the proponents' claims? Proponents argued that the state is better able to make some decisions on land use than either the federal government or localities and that public decisions are preferable to allocations in the private market. Senator Jackson argued, for example, that "In the past, land use decisions were made too often by those whose interests were selfish, short-term and private. In the future—in the face of these immense pressures on our limited land resource—these decisions must be long-term and public." What did he mean by "long-term" and what's to assure or even suggest that public decisions will be preferable to allocations in the market, that they will be anything other than an index of the relative strength of organized interests in the society?

This story, besides being an attempt to make explicit some of the assumptions that underlay the land use bill, is also the story of how "public" decisions are often made by a relatively small handful of people, people in positions of power, people who are constrained by political pressures, personal ambition, ideology, institutional responsibilities, people whose information is limited or shaped by personal experience. Understanding the forces which shaped the efforts to design national land use legislation in the early 1970's and the shortcomings of those efforts in relation to the problems to be solved, will aid in any future consideration of land use reform.

The story starts in the Senate where the first bill originated. It then moves on to the Administration's response, and then back to Congress for the final political struggle. There will be some flashbacks and side trips along the way, as ideas that helped shape the legislation are traced to their source. The motives and attitudes of the major interest groups are examined. And the paper concludes with an analysis of how the ideology, position, and attitudes of the major actors altered the structure of the bill in the legislative process and why, ultimately, the bill failed.

II. Senate Origins

The National Land Use Policy Bill that Senator Henry M. Jackson introduced in January 1970 (S. 3354) was just one of many Congressional responses to a widely perceived public anxiety about the consequences of uncontrolled growth. Other bills called for a new Congressional Office of Technology, a National Environmental Policy, a Coastal Zone Management program and an Urban Growth Policy, to name a few. As the environmental movement gathered momentum, Committees of the Congress responded, each from its own particular perspective and within the framework of Committee jurisdictional authority.

The debate over growth, whether powered by everyday concerns about pollution, congestion, the disappearance of familiar landmarks and landscapes, or by vaguer and more distant concerns about the capacity of the earth to absorb continued growth led to some particularly difficult jurisdictional conflicts in the Congress. "Quality of the environment," which became the slogan of the movement, was a concept so ill-defined and diffuse that while several Committees claimed jurisdiction, none could claim full authority to deal with the problems as they saw them. Problems cut across Committee lines of responsibility. Congressional spokesmen for resource protection programs found themselves at odds with the Committees responsible for major public works, and unable to control federal programs for highways, power dams and airports which were outside the limited range of their jurisdictional authority. Conflicts across the nation between the proponents and opponents of new highways, housing and other development were mirrored in the Congress as Committees sought to extend or protect their lines of authority and to respond to what seemed to be a widely shared environmental concern.

JACKSON STAKES HIS CLAIM

Senator Jackson's claim to share in and shape the debate over growth rested on his position as Chairman of the Senate Interior Committee. As William Van Ness, Chief Council to the Committee explains, "From Interior's perspective, the debate manifested itself in specific controversies over particular pieces of land." And land was Interior's bailiwick. Complex problems requiring mediation among transportation, housing, employment, energy and environmental policies, and among community, regional and national interests were defined in a way that brought them into the Committee's orbit of power.

Environmental issues fed the personal and jurisdictional ambitions of other senators as well. Senator Edmund Muskie of Maine, Chairman of

5

the Public Works Subcommittee on Air and Water Pollution, vied with Jackson for environmental leadership in the Senate. The most prominent environmental issues of the day—pollution and pesticides—were Muskie's issues by virtue of his subcommittee chairmanship. Jackson's claim to environmental leadership was based on a solid record of support for park and resource preservation programs throughout the 1960's, before environmental issues had assumed national prominence.

In 1969 Senator Jackson had succeeded in winning passage of the National Environmental Policy Act (NEPA).[1] Victory came at a time when environmental issues were beginning to get attention in the national press. Jackson, who had complained about the difficulty of getting the press interested in environmental issues throughout the late 1960's, was suddenly the subject of some very favorable press coverage. Jackson introduced his land use bill shortly thereafter. As one congressional analyst who worked with the Committee on the bill explained, "Bill Van Ness (Chief Counsel of the Committee) had successfully anticipated the strength of the environment as a political issue with the passage of the National Environmental Policy Act and he needed another issue to maintain the momentum gained and to keep Senator Jackson in the forefront of the environmental movement."

The first National Land Use Policy Bill, S. 3354, was introduced with rhetoric that suggested it was pro-environment. Jackson claimed, for example, that "intelligent land use planning and management provide the single most important institutional device for preserving and enhancing the environment." He also linked it closely to the National Environmental Policy Act. The title of the bill seemed to promise national policies and priorities that would somehow reconcile conflicting demands for housing, jobs, transportation and environmental protection. But the bill was not sold solely as an environmental bill. Land use planning, according to Jackson, was also the way to "maintain the material means necessary to improve the national standard of living."

The bill provided funds to the states to plan for the use of all lands (excepting land within any incorporated city with a population of over 250,000 which already had land use planning authority) and it proposed to expand the existing Cabinet level interagency Water Resources Council into a Land and Water Resources Council. State plans funded by the act would identify the areas of the state "best suited" for industry, recreation, housing and other purposes "in advance of need." These state plans,

---

1. The National Environmental Policy Act, signed into law January 1, 1970, established the Council on Environmental Quality. Section 102 of the Act requires an analysis of the impact on the environment of all major federal projects.

after receiving Council approval, were to serve as the guide to future federal programs in the states. The new Council was to maintain copies of the plans of all the states, federal agency plans and plans of local and private enterprise "to the extent practicable and appropriate." Federal agencies would be required to consult with the Council to determine "whether the proposed activity would conflict in any way with the plans of other federal, state, or local agencies."

It was a planning and coordinating bill designed, according to an Interior Committee memorandum dated April 15, 1970, to alleviate or solve the following problems: "(1) increasing pressures for conflicting uses of particular valuable land resources; (2) conflicts between environmental values and projected population and technology pressures; (3) inconsistencies in land use aims and consequences of various governmentally initiated, financed, and sanctioned projects; and (4) failure of private enterprise to consider land use consequences as a high priority factor in planning for economic growth."

The bill was troublesome in a number of respects. It was hard to match the rhetoric to the provisions of the bill and see a clear relationship between ends and means. Interest groups were decidedly not concerned that conflicts simply be resolved. They wanted to know *how* and in whose favor. A meeting between Jackson and Washington representatives of some major environmental groups which was arranged to elicit the environmentalists' support left many of those attending uncertain about what Jackson was up to. Some of them suspected the bill was designed primarily to help the power industry in its battle with local government over plant locations. The bill, despite its title, did not purport to establish national land use policy. That was a bit of hyperbole. The staff that had written the National Environmental Policy Act (which was also a procedural bill) also wrote the National Land Use Policy Act. Bill Van Ness, who was a major author of both bills, felt that the words "national policy" conveyed a sense of the bill's importance. In fact, the authors of the first land use bill considered it to be "policy neutral."

The first bill was introduced as a "working draft" and a "starting point" for discussion. As Jackson explained, "It does not purport to be a final product or to provide final answers to all the relevant questions which may be raised. It does, however, provide a starting point for review and analysis. It furnishes a working draft which federal, state, and local officials, planners, and representatives of industry, business, and public groups may comment upon."

As one of those who worked on the bill put it, "You understand, that's the way we do things up here—introduce a bill that's not fully formed as a basis for discussion. It'll be perfected as it goes through the legislative process and all the interest groups and experts get a whack at it."

The first bill was the handiwork of a few enterprising Senate Interior Committee staff members, sensitive to the emerging importance of environmental issues, eager to maintain Jackson in a position of environmental leadership, and searching for a committee role in the "growth-technology-environment" debate. They did not intend the bill to promote the interests of any particular public or private interest group, and the bill had no identifiable constituency pushing it forward. It was not the product of extensive research and analysis. It was an Interior Committee response to a whole series of vaguely understood problems, a response shaped, defined, and limited to the Committee's jurisdictional authority, anecdotal experiences of Committee members, and the background and experiences of the staff members who drafted the bill.

THE VIEW FROM THE SENATE INTERIOR COMMITTEE

The perspective that shaped Jackson's land use bill was that of a Committee with constituencies in both camps of the growth debate, a Committee with experience in public land management problems, a Committee which operated, for the most part, outside of the mainstream of urban concerns and problems. With jurisdiction over national parks and wilderness, mining and water resource development, its membership and constituency traditionally have been largely western and rural. For years the Committee acted principally to promote western water and power development and to help mining, grazing and timber interests. Although conservationists also were part of Interior's constituency because of the Committee's responsibilities for national parks and recreation, their power in relation to the development interests was relatively weak until the 1960's.

The growing strength of the environmental movement became evident between 1962 and 1967 in a number of legislative victories that Jackson helped achieve. These victories included passage of the Wilderness Act and the Wild and Scenic Rivers Act, and the creation of several new national parks, including Redwoods in California and North Cascades in Washington State.

In that decade a series of battles broke out within the Committee between the wilderness supporters and the mining interests, between the wild river advocates and the promoters of water and power development projects, between the timber interests and the park and wildlife proponents. Although these "preservationist" versus "exploiter" battles raged with intensity among a small group of special-interest advocates, they attracted little public attention. In these legislative controversies, the Committee found itself in an uncomfortable position, forced to mediate disputes between conflicting constituencies. The Committee's role was to allocate land among competing uses and these decisions were made in the political arena, outside the private market. Thus, when Jackson proposed that the states assume greater responsibility for allocating lands it was not perceived as a radical departure from existing practice. In fact, it seemed to offer a way out of some of the difficult disputes that were taking up the Committee's time and that could not be resolved to everyone's satisfaction. As Bill Van Ness explains, "The Committee found itself trying to resolve these disputes on an ad hoc, case by case basis. It was a time-consuming effort that left us no time to think about policy."

The controversy over Bridge Canyon Dam was one of those no-win situations. The Bridge Canyon Dam controversy involved plans of the Bureau of Reclamation to build a power-generating dam at Bridge Canyon on the Colorado River. The dam, which would have backed water into the Grand Canyon, aroused strong protests. The project was fought in Congress and defeated by a coalition of environmentalists brought together by the Sierra Club. In opposing the dam, the Sierra Club and others suggested that a preferable alternative was available—generation of power by steam plants. But when the steam plants were built at Four Corners, New Mexico, a new argument broke out. The giant coal-fired generating stations created significant air pollution, and the strip mining of coal reserves on Indian lands further complicated the issue.

Jackson, a supporter of the steam plant alternative in a long, bitter, highly emotional congressional fight, was outraged at the prospect of yet another battle. According to one of his staff, "This was one more example of the failure to plan intelligently, to look at all the alternatives and their ramifications, to assess the various options and their potential environmental and economic impacts. The result was a series of time-consuming, sensational battles that should have been avoided."

By the late 1960's the conflicts between preservation and development interests that previously had been fought among the Committee's constituencies took on a new dimension as highways and other public works projects began to impinge on parks, wildlife refuges, and natural areas. As citizens around the country began to resist the intrusion of highways, powerplants and other unwanted development, a new environmental constituency was born. Jackson proved an able spokesman for this new national constituency, but the conflicts presented a different kind of problem from the earlier "family" disputes. Many of these land use conflicts involved federally sponsored programs over which the Interior Committee had no jurisdiction. They pitted the Interior Committee against other Committees of Congress in situations where Interior was unable to control the outcome.

The Miami Jetport/Everglades National Park controversy typifies the jurisdictional conflicts of the Committee system where no clearcut boundaries can be established for the problems Congress tries to address. In fact, according to some Interior Committee staff members, the land use bill had its genesis in hearings the Senator held on this issue. At a minimum, the hearings dramatized some of the issues the bill was intended to address.

The Jetport controversy involved the plans of the Dade County Port Authority in Florida to build a jet pilot training facility in Big Cypress Swamp adjacent to the Everglades National Park. For some years Jackson had been fighting to protect the park in a battle that involved the allocation of water between the Park and the Miami metropolitan area. The Corps of Engineers, by means of a flood control project, manages the water supply and allocates water among the Park, agricultural users, and commercial and industrial users in southern Florida. The Interior Department, concerned that the rapidly growing greater Miami area would ultimately require a greater share of the water, wanted the Corps to establish a policy assuring that the Park would have priority should the needs of the Park and Miami come into conflict. The Corps maintained that it was up to the state to establish priorities. The fight was carried on in the Congress as well where Jackson ultimately succeeded in persuading the Public Works Committee (with jurisdiction over the Corps) to enact legislation assuring priority to the Park. Shortly thereafter, environmental groups began to publicize the Port Authority plans to build the jet training facility, plans which they maintained threatened the existence of the National Park. Jackson, continuing his efforts to protect the Park, held several days of hearings on the issue.

According to Dan Dreyfus, Staff Director of the Interior Committee and a principal author of the first land use bill, the major lesson the Committee drew from the hearings was that four different federal programs were involved in the jetport dispute (the Corps water supply program, federal aid for the airport, Interior's National Park, plus plans for a federally funded highway to the jetport) and none of the agencies knew what the others were doing. Dreyfus calls the Jetport controversy "a perfect illustration of the fact that the heavy hand of federal programs was shaping land use in the states; that conflicting, single purpose federal projects which failed to consider multiple impact were preempting logical decisionmaking by the states. No one was looking at the cumulative impact of existing federal programs and the land use conflicts inherent in competing federal programs."

The bill which Van Ness and Dreyfus drafted was intended to: (1) improve coordination of federal programs affecting land use; (2) provide money to the states to improve the technical competence of state personnel and (3) fund the development of a data base. In Dreyfus' opinion, the development of a data base was the key to resolving land use conflicts and the key to the data problem was development of a land classification system. Land classification is a familiar concept to natural resource managers, a concept that rests on analysis of inherent capability of land to perform certain functions. Agricultural land is classified in terms of its productivity on the basis of soil type, climate, rainfall, etc. In Dreyfus' opinion, "Data about the land base would give us a mechanism by which to make tradeoffs among competing land uses." Accordingly, the first bill called for massive data gathering efforts to include: (1) data on the environmental, geological, and physical suitability of land for new communities, commercial development, heavy industries, transportation and utility corridors, and other uses; and (2) data on land use requirements for recreation, urban growth, commerce, transportation, and energy generation for at least the next fifty years. Based on an analysis of these data, the states were to develop state-wide plans (excluding land within any incorporated city which already had land use planning agencies) that identified those areas of the states which were appropriate for various land uses. The State Plan would identify areas in "advance of need" and on the basis of sound information, presumably thereby avoid what the staff and Jackson called the "crisis" atmosphere surrounding land use conflicts. The notion of land classification was central to the first bill and though it was diluted as the bill went through the Congress, national land use policy proposals continued to rest on an assumption that land could be unambiguously classified as most suitable for a particular use and that data about the land base was somehow the key to allocating lands among competing uses.

Van Ness had some other ideas about how the bill would work, including an extension of the principles embodied in the National Environmental Policy Act (NEPA). That requires federal agencies to anticipate and evaluate the environmental impact of *federal* programs, but it lacks provision for evaluating the impact of *nonfederal* programs, (public and private). State land use planning, Van Ness said, would provide the vehicle for that kind of evaluation in predominantly rural areas where planning was either minimal or nonexistent. "We did not mean to weight the bill in favor of the environment," he said. "Rather, we wanted to make sure those impacts were at least considered. . . . Too many small towns are eager for anything that appears to expand the tax base. The bill was intended to open up the process and get a public debate going—to identify options and alternatives—to improve the process while making no value judgments about the outcome."

Just as the Committee's jurisdictional authority helped shape the bill, the jurisdictional problems inherent in a bill that would affect the programs of so many federal agencies deterred the staff from drawing on outside advice. It was important in the early stages to "keep a low profile," as one staff member put it, in order not to arouse suspicion that the staff was sticking its fingers into other jurisdictional pies. Since the bill was not intended to advance the interests of any particular groups, the staff also avoided the discussions with interest-group representatives. While the low profile minimized the jurisdictional problems, it also limited the Committee's pool of ideas. A group of students from MIT worked with the Committee for several months in an effort to define the problems but, according to one of the participants, their principal function was to give the effort "a patina of academic respectability."

FIRST HEARINGS

After Jackson introduced the bill in January 1970 the staff had to generate support within the Committee and find friendly witnesses, explain the bill to them, and help prepare their testimony. "The staff really had to nurse the first witnesses," one congressional analyst commented. It was not the normal kind of bill developed in response to constituent demands and it was not an easy bill to understand. Jackson and his aides viewed the hearings as a means of generating support for a general concept and a way to stimulate discussion of the issues. Jackson had meant it when he called the bill a "working draft." The staff hoped to receive suggestions for improving the bill. During the four days of hearings in 1970 the Committee heard from professional planners, federal government officials, and a few representatives from state and local governments, and private industry, and environmental groups. The witnesses were generally supportive. Most of them agreed that some kind of a bill was needed. But, as Dreyfus put it, "The hearings didn't produce a single bit of technical information to improve the bill."

The lack of controversy over the bill came as a surprise to John King, a young lawyer from Seattle, who had joined the staff in February 1970 and was assigned responsibility for the land use bill. King said his first reaction to the bill was that "it was a socialist planner's dream, and it stepped on every bureaucratic toe in town."

Diverse interest groups were willing to support the bill as long as it appeared that their particular interests would be protected. A speaker for the farmers organized in soil and water conservation districts, for example, a group that later contributed significantly to the bill's defeat in the House, was able at this stage to say that "it is becoming increasingly evident that land cannot continue to be regarded as a simple commodity in an economic jungle. . . . S.3354 seeks to provide a remedy for some of these problems and elevate the position of land as a vital resource. The National Association of Conservation Districts applauds these purposes." A panel of county executives testified in support of the county as the basic planning unit and submitted amendments to protect the county's role.

The Sierra Club raised a knotty issue—what is the "national interest," and when should it override state plans? The Sierra Club pressed for substantive guidelines that would assert the "national interest" and provide for a federal override of state decisions "when a higher environmental standard can be achieved."

The Edison Electric Institute commented that some of the findings in the Jackson bill "do not fit our experience. It is suggested that failure to conduct sound land use planning has resulted in delay and cancellations of utility development and in the location of some utility facilities without regard to relevant environmental considerations." The Institute maintained that delay was largely the result of labor problems, delays in delivery of equipment, and the lengthening of regulatory and approval proceedings. The Institute summed up its position on the bill as follows:

We agree with the need for sound land use planning and with the attempt being made in this bill to locate that function at the state level. We do not agree. . .with the assumption that current delays in utility construction will be affected in any important way by passage of S.3354. In fact, it is our opinion that the procedures suggested could well add to the already lengthy approval process required for utilities and that this would work against one of the stated purposes of the legislation.

Russell Train, then chairman of the Council on Environmental Quality, presented generally favorable testimony on behalf of the Administration. The groundwork had been laid at an earlier White House meeting arranged by Van Ness, attended by Jackson, some of his Committee's Republican members, Train, and John Ehrlichman, Assistant to the President for domestic affairs.

The issues that ultimately led to the bill's defeat in the House were raised but not pressed in the hearings. Fear of state takeover of private land without compensation, the issue that later aroused strong grassroots opposition to the bill, was not a subject of major concern. According to Steven Quarles, who joined the Interior Committee staff early in 1971 and assumed major responsibilities for the bill, "The lawyers of the Committee knew that the bill could not fundamentally affect federal and state constitutional provisions protecting private property. It simply wasn't an issue." Fear of "federal zoning," another ideological issue that contributed to the bill's defeat, was allayed by Jackson's continued insistence that "we are just suggesting that the states should exercise states rights in assuming responsibility for managing these problems." In fact, Senator Jackson resented the suggestion that the bill intruded the federal government into state business, arguing in the hearings that "here is a classic case where we have legislation in which we are not trying to specifically tell the state what to do. We are just saying, we have got statewide environmental problems that must be made compatible with our social and economic needs and you figure it out, starting at the state level, how to do it."

The Jackson bill was not improved or noticeably altered by the testimony of all the experts and interest groups. State planning was supported by a remarkably diverse group whose real interests were not compatible so long as everyone was a potential winner.

COMMITTEE ACTION

During 1970 the Interior Committee held several executive sessions on the bill. Those meetings, according to one participant, "never got down to a thoroughgoing scrutiny of the bill's provisions or its implications."

Rather than focus on details, Jackson's first order of business was to convince the Committee that land use was a politically important issue—an issue that the Committee ought to claim. According to Committee aide King, "The jurisdictional dispute with Muskie over environmental issues was beginning to heat up. Muskie had air and water. Jackson and the Committee wanted to establish Interior as the land use Committee. Jackson argued that land use was going to be a big issue. If the Committee failed to claim jurisdiction, some other Committee would assuredly move in. If that happened, the Committee would have no leverage to shape a rational program in the best interests of the nation."

The bill that was reported out of Committee on December 14, 1970, near the end of the 91st Congress was substantially the same bill that had been introduced in January.[2] States were to plan, federal programs were to be coordinated. And state plans were to guide federal activities in the states. The rules for determining allocation among competing users and competing interests were to be discovered by an analysis of resource data, the development of a land classification system, projection of needs for things like housing, power, transportation and recreation and the matching of these "needs" to the resource base. As for national policy, the Committee report had this to say, "The Committee finds a need for a national consensus upon priorities for land use. . . . The most important point on which the Committee feels the Congress should define a national consensus is the urgency of the situation."

The Committee report included a supplementary statement signed by Republican Senators Gordon Allott of Colorado and Len B. Jordan of Idaho that supported the need for a "coordinated land use system" but added

---

2. U.S., Congress, Senate, *National Land Use Policy Act* (Washington, D.C.: U.S. GPO, 1970), 91st Cong., 2d sess., 1970, S. Rept. 91-1435.

that "the issue then is not whether it should be done, but rather how it shall be done." The two senators were wary of the threat of federal intervention in state decisions implied by provisions cutting off federal funds to states that failed to comply with the legislation.[3]

Jackson's plan to bring the bill to the Senate floor for a vote shortly after Christmas was thwarted when Muskie used senatorial prerogative to put a personal hold on the bill. A story in the Washington, D.C., *Evening Star* on December 29, 1970, reported that Muskie's staff contended that the measure overlapped the jurisdiction of several other Senate committees. The article quoted a Muskie aide as saying, "Congress has not determined who has jurisdiction over land use. The Interior Committee has just assumed it. Because the committee assumed it does not mean it has the necessary jurisdiction."

Muskie opposed the Jackson bill on policy as well as jurisdictional grounds, and his objections were clarified in the next Congress when he introduced his own land use bill and several amendments to the Jackson bill which would have established specific policy objectives.

---

3. The various sanctions provisions proposed for land use policy legislation would penalize states which failed to establish planning programs by withholding federal funds for certain projects.

III. The Administration Response

Early in January 1971, shortly after the 92nd Congress convened, Jackson reintroduced his National Land Use Policy Bill, S. 632, substantially unchanged from the version reported by the Senate Interior Committee in mid-December.

Throughout 1970 Jackson had pressed the Administration to support his bill or present an alternative. Jackson had put land use legislation on the national agenda, and it was a difficult issue for the Administration to duck. Jackson was determined to keep the subject alive and as Chairman of the Interior Committee he had several opportunities to do so. In August 1970 for example, the Senate Interior Committee held oversight hearings on the Council on Environmental Quality's first annual report to the Congress. Jackson took the opportunity to publicly rebuke the Administration for its failure to submit a bill saying that he was "frankly disappointed" by the Council's response.

Furthermore, the Administration was not unaware of the environmental mood that seemed to be sweeping the country. As one White House aide explained, "The public opinion polls showed a sharp rise in public interest in environmental issues and the President ordered us to 'get out front' on the environment."

Thus, when the President sent his Environmental Message to Congress on February 8, it was accompanied by a promise that the Administration would soon submit a land use policy bill of its own. That bill, S. 992, drafted at the Council on Environmental Quality (CEQ) was submitted in late February.

The CEQ bill had the same title as the Jackson bill and, like it, called for a program of state grants. But the Administration bill was different in fundamental respects. First of all, CEQ is an agency that is an advocate for environmental interests. Jackson's concerns that industrial growth be accommodated with a minimum of social stress were not the Council's concerns. Jackson's frustrations in his dealing with federal agencies outside his Committee's sphere of influence were not shared by the Council. The basic premise of the Administration bill was that placing land use planning and control exclusively in the hands of local government was the root cause of the nation's environmental problems. The authors of the Administration bill, at least one of whom had shared the hopes and disappointments of many social planners of the 60's, were skeptics on the subject of planning, which frequently bore little relationship to policy. The key to environmental reform, they argued, lay in the power of government to regulate the use of private land. Local governments failed to use this power in the public interest, they maintained. Therefore, the Administration proposed a fundamental restructuring of governmental power, away from local government to the state, to regulate the use of private land.

THE VIEW FROM THE COUNCIL ON ENVIRONMENTAL QUALITY

The Council on Environmental Quality had been established under the provisions of the National Environmental Policy Act, which the President had signed on January 1, 1970. According to a Senate Interior Committee staffer who played a major role in developing the bill which created the Council, the Committee had intended that one of CEQ's major functions would be to provide the scientific analytical underpinnings for environmental programs. That is, CEQ was to provide the hard, objective facts needed to analyze environmental issues and move the debate beyond simple emotional response.

In February of 1970, Undersecretary of the Interior Russell Train had been confirmed as CEQ's first chairman. Train thus became the first visible high-level spokesman for environmental interests at the White House. The new CEQ chairman had impeccable credentials for his job. Train had developed an intense interest in African wildlife while serving as a federal Tax Court judge, and in 1959 he founded and became the first president of the African Wildlife Leadership Foundation. He also had served as vice-president of the U.S. World Wildlife Fund. Train's conservation activities led to an acquaintance with Laurance Rockefeller, and in 1965 Train resigned from the bench to become president of The Conservation Foundation, a Rockefeller-supported research and education organization devoted to natural resource protection and other environmental programs. Train still was with the foundation when the Administration nominated him to be Undersecretary of the Interior to clear the way for Senate confirmation of Walter J. Hickel as Interior Secretary.[1] During his short stay at Interior, Train had worked to advance federal wilderness, wild rivers, and wildlife preservation programs and he came to the Council as a strong advocate of resource protection programs.

While Congress may have hoped that CEQ would concentrate on "monitoring environmental change (and) providing environmental baseline data and other technical information," CEQ also was charged with developing presidential policy options in the environmental area at a time when environmental issues were riding a crest of public support. Train's deputy at

---

1. During Hickel's confirmation hearings, Hickel ran into heavy opposition from organized environmental groups that were doubtful of his "environmental sensitivities." In an effort to placate the hostile environmental constituency, the Administration announced that Train would serve as Undersecretary of the Interior; this cleared the way for Hickel's confirmation.

CEQ, Alvin Alm, felt strongly that CEQ should not lose itself in long-range research but should establish influence on policy by becoming identified with legislative initiatives. CEQ was only a few months old when it sought and gained responsibility for preparing the President's second Environmental Message and the legislative package that would accompany it. The Administration's land use bill was part of that package.

THE DEVELOPMENT OF CEQ'S LAND USE BILL

The land use bill was just one of several pieces of environmental legislation developed in the summer of 1970 by CEQ's small new staff, eager to capitalize on the enormous reservoir of public support for environmental protection.

An interagency task force organized by CEQ to develop the Administration's land use bill met throughout the summer. Boyd Gibbons, a lawyer who had been Train's deputy at Interior and had moved to CEQ with Train, headed the task force. Working with Gibbons was William Reilly who was one of the first to join the staff of the new Council.

The meetings of the task force were unproductive and even hostile, according to one who attended. The group was deeply divided between "the young lawyers (Gibbons and Reilly) eager to write the 'law of the land' and a small group of experienced bureaucrats who were skeptical about achieving dramatic change in land use practices through reliance on the state's power to regulate land use—whether or not a bill might be enacted."

Ultimately, it was not the task force but Gibbons and Reilly who shaped the Administration's land use policy legislation. Both agreed that the land use bill should address issues that were difficult to articulate and define. Neither of them thought the Jackson bill had much to offer. The Department of Housing and Urban Development[2] had been funding planning programs for years to little measurable effect. Both Gibbons and Reilly had arrived, by different paths, at essentially the same conclusion—the answer to environmental land reform lay in the power of the state to regulate private property. As Reilly put it in a memo which he prepared for the first task force meeting, "Land use policy must deal with two fundamental problems: (1) the inability of local government to cope with land use issues which affect the larger region, and (2) the lack of institutional machinery which combines both planning and regulatory authority." It was a solution unsupported by any convincing evidence that it would work (though there was some anecdotal

---

2. Section 701 of the Housing Act of 1954 provided planning grants for cities with a population of less than 25,000 and for metropolitan areas. Subsequently, the Act was amended to extend Section 701 to provide planning assistance for states.

evidence presented in a report prepared for the Council, *The Quiet Revolution in Land Use Control*[3] which discussed nine state or regional land use regulatory programs). It was a solution shaped by the authors' experiences, arrived at primarily because other avenues had been tried and had failed and because some solutions, namely either federal land acquisition or federally imposed restrictions on private property were not politically feasible.

Gibbons had arrived at this solution while working on the Administration's Coastal Zone bill. Reilly had come to it out of his experience as a civil rights lawyer and planner.

Coastal Zone Management. The Administration's Coastal Zone bill had been put together by a Task Force under Train's direction while Train was still at Interior. Although legislation called for "balanced use," the authors regarded it as a bill to protect coastal wetlands and open space. As one Administration official who had a hand in developing both the coastal zone bill and the later land use bill put it, "Balanced use meant a tilt toward the environment. We figured the development forces could take care of themselves."

Like the land use bill that followed, the Coastal Zone bill provided for a shift in land use planning and control from local to state governments. The bill's proponents argued that state planning was necessary to determine the coastal zone's "carrying capacity"; state planning would assure that the coastal zone would be administered for "multiple use"; the estuary is an "ecological unit" which must be managed as a whole and decisions about it must be regulated because cumulatively they may "destroy the resource." These were slogans that reinforced a position arrived at for more compelling reasons. State planning and management offered an alternative both to local regulation, which had failed to protect wetlands, and to a new federal acquisition program at a time when the Administration was committed to holding down the federal budget.[4]

The issue, according to Gibbons, was not regulation per se, but *who* should regulate, and for what *purposes.* As Gibbons explains: "We never thought of it as a public regulation versus private property issue. Rather, we

---

3. Fred Bosselman and David Callies, *The Quiet Revolution In Land Use Control* (Washington, D.C.: U.S. GPO, 1971). Prepared for the Council on Environmental Quality.

4. There were also some sound historical reasons why regulation rather than acquisition seemed an appropriate tool for coastal wetlands protection. Historically, the federal government has exercised paramount power over navigable waters and, by extension, over any private activities on land under navigable waters that might impede navigation. This unique power, known as the "navigation servitude," limits all private property rights on lands under navigable waters. Under this rule the federal government can remove private structures that might impede navigation without compensating the property owner.

Furthermore, the Corps of Engineers also has considerable regulatory authority. Under the Rivers and Harbors Act of 1899 anyone wishing to construct piers, wharves, or other structures, or to dredge and fill in navigable waters, must get a permit from the Corps. In addition to these regulatory duties, the Corps carries out massive water navigation improvement projects, usually funded 100% by the federal government.

thought in terms of which levels of govenments should do the regulation. By shifting regulatory authority from local government to the states we thought we could, at the least, prevent some of the worst abuses of local government. With their narrow concern for tax ratables they were allowing and even encouraging developers to fill and build in the wetlands. We thought the states, free of the property tax concerns, could take a broader perspective on the matter."

Regulation also was a convenient alternative to federal acquisition of wetlands. When Interior's Fish and Wildlife Service recommended a new wetlands acquisition fund separate from the coastal zone bill, the proposal was killed by Gibbons and others on the Secretary's staff. As Gibbons explained, "We knew there'd never be enough money to buy all that should be protected, and if you provide money, the states will take the easy way out."

The ALI Code. Gibbons' ideas about state land use regulation grew out of the Coastal Zone program. Reilly was to provide a different rationale. It was a rationale developed in response to the concerns, shared by many urban planners and civil rights lawyers, that local governments were using sophisticated zoning techniques to keep minorities out. It was rooted in frustration with the proliferation of regional planning agencies which had no authority to compel regional solutions to regional problems like transportation and housing. Reilly, along with other planners and land use lawyers, argued that local regulation was becoming an anachronism in a society in which many locally determined land use decisions have ramifications going beyond town boundaries. Reilly's perspective was reflected in the ALI Code, an effort to review, evaluate, and restate the body of law on public control of private development that had evolved over fifty years.[5] If adopted by state legislatures, the Code would supersede and replace the Standard State Zoning Enabling Act and the Standard City Planning Act developed by the Department of Commerce in the 1920's. These acts were adopted in some form by most states and provided the legal basis for much existing municipal land use planning and regulation.

---

5. American Law Institute, *Model Land Development Code* (Philadelphia: American Law Institute, 1974). Tentative Draft No. 6, April 15, 1974. After obtaining a law degree at Harvard and an ubran planning degree at Columbia, Reilly had joined a Chicago firm of noted land use lawyers, including Richard Babcock and Fred Bosselman, who were instrumental in developing the American Law Institute's Model Code, a monumental effort to restate and reform land use law. The Code, if adopted by the states, would (among other things) shift some regulatory authority away from local government and back to the states. Reilly was probably one of a handful of people in government who knew about the work and, more to the point, who understood its intellectual origins. Reilly also had worked for the National Urban Coalition, where along with many socially concerned lawyers in the late 1960's, he had a special interest in the open housing issue.

The regulations adopted under these acts have been sharply criticized on two fundamental grounds. First, such regulation was often ad hoc and arbitrary, not based on a community adopted plan, and not supported by any generally accepted standards. Second, local government's understanding of the public interest was so narrow that local governments avoided their social responsibility by failing to accept developments such as low cost housing needed to serve a larger community. Housing, rather than the need for natural resource protection, was the motivating concern that led the ALI to recommend that some regulatory authority be shifted back to the states and it was this perspective which Reilly brought to CEQ's efforts to evolve an Administration land use bill.

THE ADMINISTRATION'S BILL

By early September of 1970 CEQ had in hand a bill that merged ideas out of both the Coastal Zone proposal and the ALI Code. The bill was relatively simple. It provided grants to the states to encourage them to develop land use control programs to deal with a limited number of problems: (1) development in "areas of critical environmental concern" where uncontrolled development could damage "historic, cultural, or aesthetic values, natural systems or processes which are of more than local significance"; (2) areas impacted by "key facilities"—primarily growth-inducing public works projects like highways and airports; (3) large-scale development that might adversely affect neighboring communities by, for example, generating traffic and causing congestion or contributing to air and water pollution problems.

These three essentially environmental provisions were "balanced" by a requirement that states develop methods to override local decisions to exclude development needed to serve the larger region. This provision worried the environmentalists who were never sure what kind of development the authors had in mind. Many of them suspected that it might apply to energy facilities. The provision of the bill was purposely vague, referring only to "land use and private development for which there is a demonstrable need affecting the interests of constituents of more than one local government which outweighs the benefits of. . . restrictive or exclusionary local regulation." Reilly has said that low-cost housing was one category of development the authors had in mind. Reilly alerted John Ehrlichman at the White House that the bill could be interpreted so as to allow states to override exclusionary local zoning. But in this instance, as is the case with other provisions of the bill, a clear distinction must be made between what the authors of the bill had in mind and what the Administration was supporting. Though Ehrlichman and, according to Reilly, a few officials at HUD understood the implications for open housing, the bill was not sold either within the Administration or to the Congress as an open housing bill. Officials at OMB say they don't recall that the subject was ever raised.

In arguing that regulatory authority should be shifted from local government the authors were arguing a general principle that land use decisions affecting a larger region should not be made from a limited local perspective. It was a principle equally applicable to transportation, low-income housing, the location of power plants, sewage disposal plants, or regional parks. But implicit in the Administration's argument was the assumption that the practical result of applying the principle would be greater protection for the environment. The assumption was based on the belief that there was widespread public support for protecting critical areas; that states would more willingly use the police power to protect these areas than local governments that depend on land development for property tax revenues; and that local governments, unfamiliar with recent case law, were unnecessarily timid in their use of police power to protect environmental amenities: the police power could be used much more aggressively without the fear that the courts would order payment of compensation.

The proposal also was grounded on a principle of fundamental fairness: local communities should not make unilateral decisions that might adversely affect the larger region when the larger community was excluded from the decisionmaking process. Gibbons points to the Miami Jetport controversy as a classic example of an independent local decision with wide ranging effects on surrounding communities. "Disregarding the Everglades National Park aspect of the problem, it is still a good example of a decision that should not be solely a local decision," says Gibbons. But it was symptomatic of the times that the Administration bill was loaded on the side of the adverse effects that could be characterized as environmental.

OMB OBJECTS; EHRLICHMAN PROTECTS

"No one in the Administration challenged the basic philosophy of the bill—until we got to OMB," says Gibbons. "The only disputes were jurisdictional—who would get the program and what federal programs would be included in the sanctions provision."[6]

OMB had been fighting a losing battle over land use since early 1970, when CEQ wrote a letter signed by the President, that transmitted CEQ's annual report[7] to Congress. The letter said, ". . . we must work toward

---

6. The Office of Management and Budget (OMB) is the agency through which the President exercises fiscal control. New legislation is routinely reviewed by OMB prior to submission to Congress.

7. Council on Environmental Quality, *Annual Report* (Washington, D.C.: U.S. GPO, 1970), 91st Cong., 2d sess., 1970. First annual report transmitted August 1970.

development of a National Land Use Policy to be carried out by an effective partnership of federal, state, and local government together." The report and letter, Reilly said, were "like a Papal encyclical." The President had committed the Administration to develop a land use bill. The President's letter said, in part, that "traditionally, Americans have felt that what they do with their own land is their own business. . . . The time has come when we must accept the idea that none of us has the right to abuse the land, and that on the contrary society as a whole has a legitimate interest in proper land use. . . ."

This argument, however, disturbed OMB. Reilly recalls that to OMB the philosophy reflected in the letter was "fundamentally antithetical to private property and the philosophy of John Locke."

The essence of OMB's opposition, however, lay in its contention that the land use bill threatened to intrude a federal presence into issues that were constitutionally reserved to the states. This contradicted the New Federalism philosophy that power should be returned to the states from the federal government. To show that a federal interest in land use was involved, CEQ added a preamble that spelled out how federal programs affect state and local land use patterns.

In addition, OMB pointed out that the land use bill was a categorical grant program, and the Nixon Administration was committed to moving away from this approach. The Administration favored revenue-sharing, which would give state and local governments much more choice in spending federal funds.

Third, an OMB staff member explained, the Administration had just completed a two-year effort to develop a national growth policy and had concluded that a coherent policy was not possible. OMB saw land use policy as an element of growth policy and subject to the same fatal flaws.

Fourth was the problem referred to as the "indirect effect." One OMB staff member put it this way: "When you have a bill administered by a dedicated bureaucracy, that bureaucracy, with its ability to write the regulations and criteria under which the program will operate, and its power to turn the money on or off, has influence beyond the bill itself. The program becomes a fulcrum for a lot of leverage to achieve bureaucratic objectives." OMB also was concerned that the bill would "buy a lot of consultants and state planners and build a constituency hard to remove from the federal trough."

OMB was in a bind, however. The President was committed both to the New Federalism and to supporting environmental initiatives. CEQ, with strong support from the White House, was committed to a land use bill. In addition, Jackson was pressuring the Administration to take a position on his bill, which OMB regarded as an administrative nightmare that imposed unrealistic demands upon the states. OMB was willing to concede the environmentalists' argument that land use decisions were being made in a closed atmosphere; and so, while asserting that land use was not a federal responsibility, OMB agreed to support a procedural bill that would open the decisionmaking process to more citizens.

Gibbons said it required several weeks of a "substance/process" debate to overcome OMB's objections. He explains, "We'd say the states should look at development around highway interchanges. OMB would say, 'That's substance.' And we'd say, 'We're not telling them what to do, we're just saying that's a problem to be looked at.' " Gibbons and Reilly insist that little of the original proposal was lost during the exchange. Given the President's commitment to New Federalism and his general budget posture, a procedural bill was all that could have been proposed. But even had there not been the internal political problem, it is doubtful that CEQ could have written a more specific bill. The issues had not been sufficiently defined and thus, solutions were not readily apparent.

OMB's objections required resolution at the White House, where Ehrlichman overruled most of them. Gibbons and Reilly agree that Ehrlichman was the hero in the internal debate over Administration land use policy. And in fact Administration support for the land use bill is more accurately described as Ehrlichman's support. According to John Whitaker, who was then deputy assistant to the President for environment and natural resources, "When the bill first came up, the President said, 'John, you're a land use lawyer and you know what's needed. You handle the bill,' " Ehrlichman had been a land use and zoning lawyer in Seattle before joining the Administration and was not disturbed by the ideological arguments of the bill's opponents. Gibbons said Ehrilichman, however, failed to back CEQ on the major issue of sanctions, agreeing to their removal from the bill. CEQ argued that the states would not take on the political burden necessary to win back regulatory controls from local governments unless they had some powerful incentives to do so. For this reason, they proposed that uncooperative states be threatened with the loss of federal aid highway funds and other federal aid monies. But, as Gibbons explained, "Ehrlichman felt he had bloodied himself enough with the highway lobby trying to break the highway trust fund." The sanctions were out.

SUMMARY

The Administration bill went to Congress in February of 1971. The central dilemma which had confronted its authors was how to draft a bill to achieve certain environmental (and federal) policy objectives without appearing to impose federal policy on the states. Characterizing the bill as simple institutional reform was the solution needed to gain support within the Administration at a time when the Administration was committed to returning policy authority to the states. Also, one of the bill's authors said it was "the only way to get a bill through the Congress. We would never have gotten a bill that said, 'Don't develop in the wetlands; don't develop on steep slopes, etc.' "

Although the bill was sold within the Administration and to Congress as simple institutional reform that shifted some regulatory authority to the states but left them free to develop their own land use policies, the bill's authors clearly aimed at environmental ends. Gibbons says, "Environment was in the forefront as a public issue, but air and water pollution were getting all the attention. We hoped to focus attention on those environmental issues relating to protection and preservation of land." The authors wanted to focus attention because as Gibbons explains, "The environmental effects from thoughtless land development are more irreversible (sic) and more serious than those of pollution. There are technological solutions to pollution problems and solutions that do not require radical institutional power shifts."

The core of the Nixon bill was the provision requiring the states to control development in "areas of critical environmental concern." To require states to control critical areas was to imply a federal policy goal that, if met, would place limits on development in critical areas. But the nature and extent of the restrictions on private development implicit in the bill never were specified. Since the objectives were poorly explained, the nature and kind of control were left open to widely varying interpretations. Hence, even the bill's various authors and supporters disagreed about the meaning of its central provision.

The bill reflected the view of its authors that decisions about development and use of land are matters of social and political choice, and that land development historically has been subject to some community control, reflecting goals that have changed with altered social and economic conditions. The bill's authors believed that the public now would support new police power limits on development, limits aimed at protection of the natural environment. The limits of that restraint were unclear. Restraints would be set, the authors thought, by the public in each state, and the limits would depend on the strength of public support for the proposition that protection of "areas of critical environmental concern" is essential to the public welfare. The difficult question of when regulation becomes a "taking" of property (which requires that compensation be paid) would be settled by the courts, as always.

The CEQ lawyers regarded the bill as a starting point to attack problems they considered to be critically important. "We knew from the outset," Gibbons said, "that there was no consensus on goals; that there was no blanket prescription available that would be equally viable in all situations. To insist on anything more in the bill would have been stupid and presumptuous."

IV. Action by the Ninety-Second Congress 1971-72

By February 1971, early in the first session of the 92nd Congress, the major ingredients had been assembled for a debate about national land use legislation—a debate which went on for four years. Jackson had reintroduced his bill in January, and the Administration proposal followed on February 25. Neither bill aroused enthusiastic support or strong opposition throughout the 92nd Congress. In the Senate the major effort went into reconciling the Jackson bill with the Administration proposal and resolving the jurisdictional controversies that threatened to block consideration of the bill.

THE SENATE: RECONCILING THE DIFFERENCES

The differences between the Jackson bill and the Administration bill were publicly aired in letters written by Jackson and Train that appeared in *The Washington Post* in late 1971. The exchange was touched off by a *Post* editorial in support of the Jackson bill which had this to say:

Senator Jackson's bill calls for comprehensive statewide planning based on over-all economic, social and environmental concerns. It challenges the planners to assure a brighter future by bringing our economic and social needs into balance with the requirements of the natural environment. The Administration's bill would have the state plans focus only on "areas of critical environmental concern" or "regional benefit," and this seems to us only a call to put out the brush fires.[1]

Train responded with a letter to the *Post* laying out the Administration's position.

. . . First, we have somewhat less faith than you in the efficacy of "comprehensive planning." We are not impressed by the results of comprehensive planning in most cities. We are not interested in encouraging more "advisory planning. . . ."

Second, we do not want to force all states to take more control from their local governments than is absolutely necessary to deal with regional or statewide land use issues. . . .

Finally, . . .our bill would require states to establish a process to permit "development of regional benefit" to be weighed against a locality's reasons for wanting to exclude such development. . . . the Administration's land use bill goes beyond planning to the central issue of controls. It is at this point that our legislation is quite specific indeed, calling for a fundamental reallocation of responsibilities between state and local governments where regional issues are involved.[2]

---

1. *Washington Post,* 20 November 1971, editorial.
2. *Washington Post,* 15 December 1971, letter to the editor from Russell E. Train, Chairman, Council on Environmental Quality.

Jackson responded with a letter[3] criticizing the Administration bill as a "labels approach" which precluded careful consideration and integration of all relevant social, economic, and environmental concerns and a prejudging of land use without adequate study."

In fact, Jackson and the Administration had different objectives and were operating on very different premises and assumptions. Jackson was looking for a way to help resolve controversies over the use of land. In his opinion, the controversies arose because single-purpose federal agencies failed to consider the environmental implications of their actions when they built highways and dams and other projects. In addition, states failed to anticipate and plan for future needs. Finally, Jackson believed, a multitude of federal, state, and local projects were being planned in a vacuum, and, somewhere down the road, were bound to cause trouble when several different agencies revealed their designs on a particular piece of land. Thus the Jackson bill emphasized future planning and contained complex administrative provisions aimed at coordinating a bewildering number of federal, regional, state and local actions. The state plan was to be the final place of resolution since all federal programs (except in the case of "overriding national interest") would have to be consistent with the state plan.

The Administration bill, on the other hand, was aimed at somewhat more limited development and preservation objectives: protection of critical areas and developments of regional benefit. The fundamental premise of the Administration bill was that local land use regulation was the problem.

The Committee Solution. The Senate Interior Committee held four days of hearings on the two bills early in the spring of 1971. Following these hearings a new bill, S. 632 was put together by Interior staff member Quarles. Quarles, a young lawyer who had served as social science program coordinator for the Ford Foundation in Brazil, had come to the Committee on the recommendation of the Ford Foundation's environmental staff. Quarles was given a free hand to produce a compromise bill. He was uniquely suited to the task. As a member of the Interior Committee staff he understood the problems and the perspective that has shaped Jackson's original bill. He shared Jackson's belief that, as Quarles put it, "Ninety percent of the conflict problems are procedural; better information and more public involvement will handle a large measure of the difficulties." He understood Jackson's concern that something be done to "get the federal house in order, and that both direct federal construction programs and federal grant programs are powerful determinants of state land use patterns." Quarles also shared with Reilly a knowledge of land use law and the historical evolution

3. *Washington Post,* 28 December 1971, letter to the editor from Henry M. Jackson, Chairman, U.S. Senate Committee on Interior and Insular Affairs.

of land use controls. He had read the same books, studied the same cases, argued the same issues. Thus not long after joining the Committee he was able to write a Committee report, discussing the history of land use controls that Washington columnist David Broder praised as a masterpiece of professionalism.

The bill Quarles put together was not a compromise (impossible to do with such fundamentally different bills). It was a combination of the earlier Jackson bill and the Administration proposal.

The new bill, which was reported in June (S. Rept. 92-869),[4] contained what the report described as "the most realistic and sound of the provisions" from both earlier proposals. It provided funds for a three-year state planning effort to be followed by grants for two years to develop state land use programs. The planning provisions were similar to the earlier Jackson bill: inventory of state land, data on population, projections of land needed and suitable for recreation, agriculture, mineral development, forestry, industry, commerce, energy development, transportation, urban development, economic diversification, rural development, etc.; an inventory of environmental, geological, and physical conditions which influence the desirability of various types of land use. In addition the states were to develop methods to inventory large-scale development, land use of regional benefit, and areas of critical environmental concern.

After three years of planning, the states were to develop methods to control development in areas of critical environmental concern; areas impacted by key facilities, large-scale development and for overriding local controls that include development of regional benefit.

To deal with the "federal problem," the bill provided that a National Advisory Board on Land Use Policy be established. The Board, made up of high level representatives of federal agencies which have programs with significant land use impact, was to advise the Secretary of the Interior (who was awarded jurisdiction of the program in the new bill) and serve the coordinating function that had been assigned to the Land and Water Resources Council in the earlier Jackson bill.

The new bill, said one CEQ staffer, "had all our guts and all Jackson's embroidery." But in Quarles' estimation, the planning requirements (absent from the Administration bill) would produce the information on which to base the decisions about what should be protected and what should be developed.

A note in a later Committee report elaborated on the relationship of the "planning process" to the "land use program."

---

4. U.S., Congress, Senate, *Land Use Policy and Planning Assistance Act of 1972: Report Together With Minority and Additional Views to Accompany S. 632* (Washington, D.C.: U.S. GPO, 1972), 92d Cong., 2d sess., 1972, S. Rept. 92-869.

A principal objective of S.268 is to encourage preparation of State land use programs. Clearly, total acre-by-acre, activity-by-activity planning at the State level, providing for all of the detailed needs of society, would be undesirable and impossible—both financially and politically.

On the other hand, the Committee believes that it is the very essence of the land use concept that a measure of comprehensiveness be included in planning. The aim is to have a real knowledge of the available resource—all of it.

S.268, borrowing from the Model Land Development Code devised by the American Law Institute, asks the States to assume authority over only that 10% of decisions which comes under the five categories of critical areas and uses which are clearly of more than local concern. Certainly, such an approach allows a minimum of State intervention in local affairs; but without a comprehensive overview such a critical areas and uses approach may be nothing more than "spot zoning" at the State level. Without an adequate understanding of the entire land resource, the State land use program will constitute a re-inventing of the so-called "zoning game" at the State level. The land use decisions embodied in the State land use program will be based on nothing more than short-term "hunch" and immediate political pressure.[5]

Thus, the fundamentally different approaches of the two bills were joined. The authors of the Administration bill saw the issue as a simple realignment of power interests which presumably would strengthen environmental controls. Jackson wanted to focus power to deal with conflict but, speaking not as an advocate for either side, thought better information would raise the level of the debate and the resulting decisions.

The crucial piece of information, as in the earlier Jackson bill, was knowledge of the "entire land resource." But in the new bill the old land classification concept which Dreyfus had proposed as the basis for making trade-offs was discarded for a new rule with strong environmental overtones. "Carrying capacity"—the amount of development that a natural system can sustain—would provide the key to determining how much and what kind of development should be permitted.

Debate in the 92nd. The bill reached the floor in September 1972 and, with a minimum of debate, was passed by a vote of 60-18. Several amendments were adopted on the floor. Some of them had been requested by local governments which, in return for their support, wanted stronger provisions for local participation in future state planning. The net effect of the amendments was to compromise the Administration's basic objective of shifting regulatory authority from local government to state government.

Much of the debate was on several amendments the Committee had accepted in order to resolve jurisdictional disputes. The Banking Committee

5. U.S. Congress, Senate, Committee on Interior and Insular Affairs, *Land Use Policy and Planning Assistance Act: Report Together With Minority and Additional Views to Accompany S. 268* (Washington, D.C.: U.S. GPO, 1973), 93rd Cong., 1st sess., 1973, S. Rept. 93-197, p. 97.

was appeased with an amendment that gave the Department of Housing and Urban Development a role in reviewing state plans. The Public Works Committee got an amendment providing that state plans would be drawn in a way that would uphold the supremacy of federal air and water pollution control standards. The Coastal Zone Management Program, under the jurisdiction of the Commerce Committee, was assured an independent existence.

The only major criticism of the bill came from Muskie, who charged that it "creates an outline for national land use policy with no substance; declares a national policy but concedes to the several states responsibility to determine what that policy shall be and directs all federal programs to subject themselves to the states' determined policy." Muskie said that his objections were well expressed in a letter to *The New York Times* written by a former Public Works Committee staff member.

Perhaps Mr. Train believes that the development of flood plains is poor land use, that loss of agricultural land to sprawl is poor land use, that rapid loss of wetlands is poor land use. Perhaps Mr. Train feels that open space per capita must be increased. But unless Congress establishes these as policy, the federal bureaucracy will be helpless in the face of competing economic forces that are deeply rooted in our social fabric. I find nothing in the bill to justify your conclusion (a *Times* editorial) that it will "safeguard a growing nation's rapidly diminishing resources." A bill simply entitled "National Land Use Policy" does not ensure coming to grips with the issues directing the destiny of the nation.[6]

Muskie offered several amendments during the debate that would have provided specific federal standards for land use. His amendments proposed, for example, that productive agricultural land should be preserved for farming activities, except where there were overriding needs for housing; that wetlands and coastal areas should be protected from development; and that development should not be allowed in flood plains. He also argued that proposals for major land use reform had to deal with the issue of local dependence on the property tax. The Muskie amendments were not debated. The environmentalists did not support them because they would have killed the bill. The Administration could not support the amendments or any other substantive policies, having agreed to a land use bill on the premise that it remain a procedural bill. The Interior Committee was not willing to agree that Muskie's policies should be universally applied across the nation. The Muskie approach was much like the Administration's "spot-zoning" approach. Before one could make those decisions, more information (planning) was needed. The need for and definition of national policies was to be the subject of considerable debate in the 93rd Congress.

---

6. *New York Times*, 28 August 1972, letter to the editor from Thomas C. Jorling, Minority Counsel (1969 to June 1972) to U.S. Senate Committee on Public Works.

THE HOUSE: OTHER PRIORITIES PREVAIL

Although the land use bill passed the Senate easily, it received little attention in the House. Rep. Wayne Aspinall, chairman of the House Interior Committee, was more interested in his own bill aimed at asserting congressional influence in the management of federal lands. Although both Jackson and Administration bills were introduced in the House, Aspinall argued that Congress should "get its own house in order" before dealing with planning for nonfederal lands.

In the early 1960's Aspinall had introduced the legislation which resulted in the creation of the Public Land Law Review Commission, which was charged with a review of the laws, regulations, and administrative practices that had accumulated over many decades to govern the use of federal lands. Management of the public lands was not an insignificant issue, since those lands include the national parks and forests, national wildlife refuges, Indian reservations, and 450 million acres of public domain lands managed by the Interior Department's Bureau of Land Management. In all, the federal government owns one-third (or more than 700 million acres) of all land in the continental United States, including about half of the land west of the Mississippi River.

On June 23, 1970, the commission issued its final report.[7] Subsequently, Aspinall introduced his bill, which called for congressional review of all the public lands that had been withdrawn from the public domain by Executive Order to create national forests, national monuments, and other reservations. The bill also contained elaborate machinery for classifying public lands according to their dominant use.

Aspinall's bill was another step in his long-term effort to retrieve for Congress authority that he believed to have been relinquished to the Executive Branch. The bill alarmed conservationists, who had fought hard to have the lands in question set aside permanently. They saw the bill as a means for overturning their hard-earned victories.

Because it was opposed by the Administration, Jackson, and the environmentalists, Aspinall's bill did not have much chance of success. In late December 1971 Aspinall decided, on the advice of his staff, to combine his public lands bill with Jackson's national land use bill. This would force Senate consideration of the public lands proposal and provide room for some trade-offs with opposing conservationists. "The House Interior Committee preferred Jackson's comprehensive planning approach, but was willing to accept the Administration's critical areas approach that now was part of

---

7. U.S. Public Land Law Review Commission, *One Third of the Nation's Land* (Washington, D.C.: U.S. GPO, 1970), 91st Cong., 2d sess., 1970. Report transmitted June 1970.

Jackson's bill," said Charles Conklin, staff director of the Committee and principal staff member of Aspinall's Environment Subcommittee.

The struggle in the House through 1971-72 was mostly a battle between economic interests and preservationists over the public lands question. The House Interior Committee on August 7, 1972, reported a combined land use planning and federal lands bill. The bill remained bottled up in the House Rules Committee for the rest of the session. In an election year the bill raised issues which Congress preferred to avoid. In addition, Congressman Aspinall was then involved in a bitter primary election battle with a candidate who was running as an environmentalist. A floor debate on the Public Lands bill would not have helped him overcome the charge that he was "anti-environment."

During most of the 92nd Congress the organized conservation groups concentrated their efforts on defeating the bill, a bill so odious to them that they would readily have sacrificed the national land use bill to defeat it.

INTEREST GROUPS AND ISSUES: THE 92ND CONGRESS

The land use planning bill that passed the Senate in September 1972 had the nominal support of the governors, county and local government, the environmental lobby, and some developer interests. Most observers perceived it as a relatively innocuous piece of "good government" legislation that threatened no one and had unassailable purposes (rational land use planning). Most of the opposition rested on a general conservative stance against any new federal program and vague apprehensions that the bill opened the door for federal zoning.

But the environmentalists, despite their nominal support, were confused about how their interests would be affected by the bill and divided in their assessment of its effects. Though it seemed intended as environmental legislation, the bill failed to translate that intention into specific national policies. The environmentalists pushed for national environmental standards similar to those proposed by Muskie in 1972. Quarles resisted, arguing that it would be impossible to get any agreement on standards, that the issues were too localized to lend themselves to national standards, and that the environmentalists should take their case to the states. But he agreed to consider the national policy question in the next Congress and urged the environmentalists to get together to try to develop some recommendations.

The bill's emphasis on long-range balanced planning and institutional reform failed to arouse much grassroots interest among local conservation and environmental organizations. The mining, timber, and electric utility industries, and the trade associations for the housing and real estate interests, were equally confused about what would be the best stance for them to take on the bill. Convinced that as a vaguely environmental bill the legislation was unbeatable, these interests preferred to take a "let's be constructive" stance. Rather than outright opposition, they worked for amendments to protect their positions.

Oddly, none of the developer interests, with the exception of a lobbyist for the National Association of Electric Companies (NAEC) seems to have grasped the bill's full potential as a mechanism for state siting of major development. While representatives of several trade organizations pressed for recognition of their particular interest in the planning section of the bill, the NAEC went beyond, winning a Committee amendment which defined energy facilities as a "critical use" subject to state control. It was this amendment that confirmed the suspicions of some environmentalists that Jackson's motivations were pro-power and that contributed to a decision that brought David Calfee of the Environmental Policy Center (a Washington-based environmental lobby) into the game. Calfee was to assume a key role as the lobbyist for environmental interests in the debate over national land use policy.

V. Action by the Ninety-Third Congress 1973-1974

If anything, the prospects for a national land use planning act should have been better than ever in 1973. Environmentalists had closed out 1972 with a stunning victory, a substantial override of the President's veto of the massive water pollution control bill. Earlier in the year the veteran Aspinall had gone down to defeat in the Colorado primary elections. Morris Udall, who succeeded to the chairmanship of the House Environmental Subcommittee, was a champion of environmental legislation.

REPEAT IN THE SENATE

The bill that had passed the Senate so easily in September 1972 was reintroduced in virtually identical form, (S. 268) in January of 1973. Several hearings were held, and the bill was reported out of committee at the end of May.

The Committee report[1] discussed at length the issue of whether or not the bill should include national land use policies. The issue had been addressed by several witnesses during the hearings and though a number of them ranging from a spokesman for Exxon Company, USA, to the Conservation Foundation, argued that the bill should contain a statement of national policy, there was no agreement on the substance of such a policy or set of policies.

The Committee report laid out the argument for and against:

Without national policies, national interests such as national security, energy supply, environmental protection, etc., could be frustrated by conflicting policies adopted by the states, policies which could develop indirectly through inference and regulations adopted to administer the Act.

On the other hand, the Committee agreed, the diversity of land resources across the nation militates against a national approach, the record of European countries which have adopted land use policies is not encouraging and officially. . . "there is virtually no consensus on the possible substance of national land use policies."

The report concludes:

The Committee gave careful consideration to these and other arguments for and against national land use policies. Particular weight was given to the lack of sufficient knowledge concerning or a consensus on either the feasibility or the substance of national policies; to the danger of administrative adoption, by inference or

---

1. U.S., Congress, Senate, Committee on Interior and Insular Affairs, *Land Use Policy and Planning Assistance Act: Report Together With Minority and Additional Views to Accompany S. 268* (Washington, D.C.: U.S. GPO, 1973), 93rd Cong., 1st sess., 1973, S. Rept. 93-197.

regulation, of national policies in the absence of Congressional action; and to the need, if such policies are determined to be appropriate, to formulate them expeditiously so as to give early guidance to the States in developing their land use programs.

The solution was an amendment which the Committee adopted providing for a three year feasibility study of national land use policies to be carried out by the Council on Environmental Quality, with participation by the Interagency Advisory Board, the states and local governments.

According to the report:

The Committee believes that this study will generate the necessary knowledge and, if not establish a consensus, at least focus the issues sufficiently to allow a Congressional determination of whether national policies are appropriate and, if so, what they should be.

The reported bill also contained a new and ultimately controversial amendment designed to control the second-home industry. The Amendment had been suggested by Senator Gaylord Nelson of Wisconsin. It was drafted by Quarles, John Heritage, a Nelson staffer, and David Calfee, a lobbyist with the Environmental Policy Center. Introduction of the amendment led many observers to perceive land use legislation as primarily intended to stop the second-home industry.

Nelson introduced the amendment by blaming the industry for causing a "resource tragedy of unprecedented proportions." He called the "explosion of massive real estate developments. . . an epidemic of land development that is threatening nearly every remaining scenic area in this country." The amendment *required* the states to regulate the second-home industry under very specific criteria. Second homes could be developed only if the developer showed proof of financial capability, and the project would not cause unreasonable soil erosion, would not be located in a flood plain, would not place an unreasonable burden on local governments to produce services, and would not unreasonably damage the area's natural beauty.

According to Quarles, though the amendment violated the "no federal interference" principle, the Committee, including some of the most conservative members, were willing to accept it at a time when fraudulent or highly questionable mail order land sales and land development schemes were capturing the headlines. Quarles remembers that one of the Committee's most conservative members said at the time, "Who wants to be put in the position of having voted for Boise Cascade?"

After two days of debate the bill passed easily on June 21, by a vote of 64 to 21. The Administration still was supporting the bill. The President had called it his highest environmental priority in the State of the Union message. The opposition was lying low. As Dan Denning of the U.S. Chamber of Commerce explained: "Jackson had the votes in the Senate. The grassroots hadn't been mobilized. I decided, why spill blood in the Senate. Better to lie back and wait for the bill in the House."

DEFEAT IN THE HOUSE

Although the members of both the Environment Subcommittee under Udall and the full House Interior Committee now were weighted on the environmental side, land use legislation did not have smooth sailing. The Committee's calendar was jammed with new legislative proposals as a result of the energy crisis, and Udall's Environment Subcommittee also was trying to deal with the thorny problem of surface mining regulation. As 1973 wore on, environmental considerations were displaced by concerns about energy supply in the minds of many members of Congress.

Subcommittee Action. During March and April of 1973 the Environment Subcommittee held hearings on several different versions of the land use legislation, including the Senate and Administration versions. For the rest of the summer the Subcommittee grappled with several important and knotty issues, but it did not arrive at many firm conclusions. The bill that was reported to the full Committee was, in essence, the same bill the Senate had passed in June. A greatly modified public lands section was added, along with provisions for coordinating federal and state plans that had been recommended by the Public Land Law Review Commission. Also included was a provision similar to the Nelson amendment in the Senate, to require states to regulate second-home development.

But nobody had firm answers for the really tough questions.

—Should the bill establish a national policy? If so, what should the substance of such a policy be?

—Should federal review go to the substance of a state plan or simply to assuring that an adequate planning process existed? Didn't substance imply federal interference, which would upset the Administration and conservatives generally?

—How should environment be defined? Did it mean only ecological considerations, or other social and economic needs as well?

Opposition Rises. As the full House Interior Committee began consideration of the bill in September, the first signs of significant opposition began to appear. After probing the bill for months, Dan Denning of the U.S. Chamber of Commerce had concluded that the measure was not merely an attempt at balanced planning and institutional reform, with federal review limited to procedural matters. Denning decided, instead, that the bill contained federal guidelines that would lead to federal control of land development, that it threatened private property rights, and that it was, in essence, an *antigrowth* bill.

Subsequently, Denning sought to arouse opposition to the bill through newsletters and pamphlets issued by the Chamber and sent to its members, and by discussions with Washington representatives of various commercial, industrial, and housing associations. Along with the Chamber, the ultra-conservative Liberty Lobby launched a major effort to defeat the bill.

As a result, many members of Congress for the first time began to receive a substantial amount of mail on the bill. Many letters charged that the bill infringed on private property rights and would lead to federal intervention in local land use decisions. On October 16, Udall and Congressman Philip E. Ruppe of Michigan, the chief Republican spokesman for the bill on the committee, sent a "Dear Colleague" letter to their 433 fellow members. Udall said some letter writers had suggested that the bill would permit the federal government to take a person's land upon his death, or that it would "give known thieves and criminals and specifically rustlers legal rights to camp all summer in a pasture with an abundant supply of his choice beef."

Despite the growing opposition Udall and his staff remained confident during the fall of 1973 that the bill would reach the floor and be passed. The Interior Committee rejected a number of attempts to postpone consideration of the bill, and Udall and environmental lobbyists agreed to modify the bill's provisions for regulation of subdivisions and second-home communities. The Administration had argued that the provisions made it hard to defend the bill as a mere procedural measure that left all of the important decisions to the states, and the Administration was committed to a procedural bill.

Then, on November 7, Congressman Sam Steiger, a Republican member of the committee from Arizona, introduced a different version of the land use bill. Steiger's bill, drafted with Denning's help, contained no provisions dealing with areas of critical environmental concern or uses of more than local concern.

Nonetheless, President Nixon again called for enactment of the Committee's land use legislation in his State of the Union message on January 20, 1974. Two days later the House Interior Committee rejected the Steiger substitute and voted 26-11 to report the Committee's land use bill to the House floor. It appeared that a *pro forma* request to the Rules Committee would clear the bill for consideration by the full House. Udall asked for a very reasonable rule, one that would permit a House vote on both the Steiger substitute and the Committee bill.

Surprise in the Rules Committee. Udall confidently presented his case for the Committee's bill at a February 26 hearing of the Rules Committee. He recalled for Rules Committee members that the Senate had passed the bill overwhelmingly in 1973 and that it had the endorsement of President Nixon. But Steiger told the Committee that the President no longer endorsed the Interior Committee bill. According to Steiger, he had persuaded President Nixon to change his mind during a February 6 meeting at the White House. House Majority Leader John J. Rhodes also told the Rules Committee that the President no longer supported the Interior Committee version and preferred the Steiger substitute. Rhodes added, however, that the Administration "is not prepared to say that the committee bill is completely repugnant, and that it would support the committee bill if the substitute was not agreed to."

But Steiger was playing for keeps. If his substitute were defeated, he argued, the Interior Committee bill would have a good chance of passing. Steiger said he would prefer not to have any bill rather than risk passage of the Committee version. Throughout the hearing Rules Committee members complained that environmentalists had delayed construction of the trans-Alaskan Pipeline, refineries, power plants, and reclamation projects. Steiger told the Rules Committee that the Interior Committee's bill—like NEPA before it—would give environmentalists further latitude for litigation. Congressman B. F. Sisk of California then offered a motion to delay action indefinitely. "I'd like to kill it right here and send it back to committee," he said. "We should use whatever methods at hand to defeat it."

The Rules Committee voted 9-4 to delay consideration of the bill indefinitely. It was a major, unanticipated setback for Udall and the proponents of the bill. Critics charged that Udall had failed to do his homework. He had not thought it necessary to lobby the Rules Committee where the bill's opponents had been quietly at work urging the bill's rejection. Udall seemed utterly surprised both by the report of the President's change of position and by the Rules Committee action.

REVIVAL AND DEFEAT

After the Rules Committee setback Udall held a series of hearings to give opponents of the legislation a chance to air their views, since the Rules Committee had focused on Steiger's complaint that the opposition had been given no opportunity to comment on the bill. In addition, Jackson interceded with Ray Madden, Rules Committee chairman. Although Udall did not change the bill after the hearings, he did agree to offer several amendments on the floor. In May the Rules Committee voted 8-7 to send the land use bill to the House floor under a rule calling for a vote on the Steiger substitute before consideration of the Committee version.

The issue before the House on June 12, 1974, was whether the rule permitting debate should be accepted. The House voted 211-204 to reject the rule. Land use legislation was dead in the 93rd Congress.

That same day Jackson and Udall called a press conference to denounce the waffling of the White House. They charged that impeachment politics and right-wing scare tactics had defeated the bill. Jackson and Udall said that President Nixon had originally backed the bill but changed his position to gain conservative support in his effort to escape impeachment over the Watergate affair. However, when asked directly by reporters, Udall said he had no evidence that the President had abandoned the land use bill to gain support in the impeachment struggle.

During the House debate the opponents claimed the bill would permit the taking of private property without compensation and that it would open the door for federal bureaucrats to begin controlling land use decisions that belonged to state and local governments. But Congressman Don H. Clausen of California went to the heart of the problem with the legislation: "During the past few months the debate surrounding the Udall bill and the Steiger substitute has made clear two facts. First, there is no consensus on the subject in regard to the specifics of the legislation or the final outcome it will create. Second, there is a lack of understanding as to the impact the bill will have."

In fact, the opposition had been laying the groundwork for defeat for more than a year. And when the hour of voting arrived, circumstances gave the opponents new allies. The economy was in trouble, people were worried about energy supplies, and the inevitable backlash against overly ambitious and poorly drawn environmental legislation had begun to set in. Furthermore, the Administration's position had become extremely confusing as its attention was diverted by the problem of Watergate, which caused Ehrlichman's departure from the White House early in 1974. His absence had an immeasurable effect. As Whitaker explains, "With Ehrlichman gone, there wasn't anyone around to take up the defense."

VI. An Analysis of the Bill's Defeat

Failure to include national environmental standards had left the land use bill's natural constituency, the environmentalists, uncertain during the 92nd Congress whether the bill had anything to recommend it. Their dilemma is evident in a memo prepared in January 1973, early in the 93rd Congress, for a group of environmentalists who met over a period of several months to discuss strategy in dealing with the bill. Advised that Quarles of the Senate Interior Committee saw no prospect for adding substantive criteria to the bill and that the Committee had decided to stick with a procedural bill, one member of the group wrote:

Past experience with environmental legislation, and as environmentalists we clearly ought to see this as environmental legislation even if Jackson does not, seems to raise significant doubt about such a strategy. In both air and water pollution, we began with procedural legislation, found that over relatively long periods of time it didn't help, and finally moved in a substantive direction. . . . To avoid similar problems in the field of land use legislation, it is at least essential that the procedures which are established by the bill be those which, if we were fighting for substantive criteria, we would support as a means of implementing those criteria. Is the Jackson bill such a bill? No one seems to know.[1]

The bill's failure to elicit the enthusiastic support of the environmental community puzzled and disappointed CEQ staff, who concluded that the bill's natural proponents failed to grasp the potential for land use reform implicit in the states' police power. As early as 1971 CEQ had published Bosselman and Callies' study, *The Quiet Revolution in Land Use Control,* which described nine statewide and regional land use regulatory programs. In an effort to educate the environmentalists CEQ also sponsored a study which explored the constitutional limits of public regulation, discussed changing concepts of private property rights, and frankly advocated an extension of public control over private property for environmental ends. This study, *The Taking Issue,*[2] along with the report *The Use of Land,*[3] supported by Laurance Rockefeller funds and written by a task force under the direction of Reilly, may have won some converts to the bill. If so, it was at the expense of alerting and arousing the opposition and providing them with

---

1. Zero Population Growth, January 29, 1973. Untitled Memorandum.
2. Fred Bosselman, David Callies, and John Banta, *The Taking Issue: A Study of the Constitutional Limits of Governmental Authority to Regulate the Use of Privately Owned Land without Paying Compensation to the Owners* (Washington, D.C.: U.S. GPO, 1973). Sponsored by the Council on Environmental Quality.
3. William K. Reilly, ed., *The Use of Land: A Citizen's Policy Guide to Urban Growth* (New York: Thomas Crowell Co., 1973).

more of the ammunition they needed to conduct a major grassroots campaign against the bill. The bill's opponents charged that behind all the rhetoric about balanced use and institutional reform was a plot to extend the leviathan state and eliminate the rights of private property owners.

But the argument over public regulation was not solely ideological. It was also, in large measure, economic. The opponents perceived regulation as an antigrowth ploy, as a tool to further aesthetic and elitist objectives. Denning complained: "Those guys get upset when they see a trailer park in a scenic valley. They ought to go down into Appalachia and see how those people lived before they could afford a trailer." Gibbons, on the other hand, framed the issue this way: "Why should some developer be allowed to dredge and fill. . . and permanently destroy a productive wetland. . . to build some vacation homes and get rich?" The land use debate revolved around these related issues. But it never came into focus because the policy ends and the social and economic costs and benefits of public regulation never were made explicit or debated.

The other major issue—the feared threat of federal zoning or federal interference in local land use decisions—met with varying responses, which depended on whether the federal presence was perceived as strengthening the forces pushing for natural resource protection. The environmentalists urged national standards as long as the issue was environmental standards but opposed any federal role that implied help to the developers. The proponents of economic growth and development opposed environmental standards, but many would have endorsed federal intervention for specific purposes, such as siting energy facilities. Most often, local control was an argument of convenience. In the absence of any agreement over ends, the opponents charged, with some truth, that the federal agency that controlled the purse strings would control the policy.

Positions on the land use bill shifted as perceptions of the bill's intent and effect changed and as the political climate moved from enthusiasm for environmental issues to concern about the economy. The bill was supported by some strange bedfellows—the environmentalists and the National Association of Realtors, for example, but the support of both was always fragile. Much so-called support was, in fact, an agreement not to work for defeat of the bill in exchange for concessions. It was a strategy dictated, in part, by the assumption that some kind of bill was certain to pass. Interest-group positions on the bill usually reflected the views of the Washington lobbyists rather than their constituents. As the grassroots opposition was organized, land use became an ideological issue. Among the lobbyists support and opposition reflected pragmatic evaluations of the bill's economic effects, of its strength as an environmental bill, and of its effect on traditional power relationships.

In the final analysis, the bill's fate was strongly influenced by only a few of these men. For them the bill was also a vehicle for extending power and influence, the debate, a national forum for projecting personal philosophies and pursuing a mixture of private and public ends. Two of them, David Calfee, who spoke for the environmentalists, and Denning, who mobilized the opposition, were among the few who had the resources, the time, and the willingness to work hard to strengthen or scuttle the bill.

THE ENVIRONMENTAL LOBBY: A ONE-MAN SHOW

Generally, the grassroots environmental organizations paid little attention to the land use bill. The environmental position was defended by David Calfee, former Naderite who joined the staff of the Environmental Policy Center in January 1973. His first assignment was to monitor the land use bill to make sure it did not become, as Calfee says, "a vehicle for the energy producers to rape the land."

The able and hard-working Calfee soon was busy trying to strengthen the land use bill's environmental thrust. His attention to detail and understanding of the bill made Calfee the spokesman for environmental concerns in the land use debate. Calfee was effective because he not only worked hard, but refused to make unreasonable demands. For example, he shunned Muskie's national environmental standards, believing they would lead to defeat of the bill.

The environmentalists rejected Jackson's premise that the policy-neutral planning provisions of the bill automatically would lead to land use decisions that were environmentally sound. In the words of Calfee, "There is no such thing as a planning principle. It's all a matter of power." But planning did offer environmentalists an opportunity to enlarge their role in the process of making decisions about land use. Calfee and the environmentalists therefore worked hard to strengthen the public participation provisions of the bill.

On the other hand, Calfee and the environmentalists thought that the bill's other goal, institutional reform, offered them little in the absence of a statement of environmental policy objectives. The experience of the environmentalists was that whenever the states made final land use decisions, the states ruled in favor of land development. Convinced that national environmental standards were unattainable, Calfee successfully pressed for a provision to require states that adopted land use plans to consider certain federal guidelines, including those on the aesthetic and ecological values of wetlands, the value of watershed land for storing and retaining water, and the cost of development in the flood plain. This provision would give environmentalists some leverage when the states began to develop their land use plans.

Although the provision does not seem particularly forceful, environmentalists regarded it as the key to success in the states and their major reason for supporting the bill. "The environmentalists really felt that it was important to get that in, though I don't know why," said Charles Conklin, staff director of the House Interior Committee.

Calfee, a Yale-trained lawyer (where he had been a classmate of Steve Quarles), had a clear grasp of the bill's potential and limitations as a vehicle for encouraging more aggressive regulatory programs. Where sound arguments could be made on grounds of economics, or health and safety, or perhaps ecology, state regulation of private property might be upheld by the courts. But, as Calfee noted in a memo commenting on the bill:

Since the police power regulation must constitutionally be "reasonably related to health or welfare" it will be limited to mechanisms, like subdivision regulations, to improve the quality of run-off, erosion and similar problems. It is clear that the Act provides no mechanism and no encouragement for preserving open space or prohibiting development, which even though regulated, will obliterate the particular features of these environmentally sensitive areas which make them worth preserving.

As Calfee explains, "The police power is a weak reed if your objective is aesthetics."

Calfee worked not only to get environmentalist language into the bill, but also to remove language he thought harmful. During the Senate debate in the 92nd Congress, the electric utility industry had succeeded in inserting a reference to energy facilities in the section of the bill providing for state control of key facilities. The provision could have given the states authority for siting energy facilities in the face of local opposition. Early in the 93rd Congress, another small but potentially significant change was made—states would have to consider "the national interest involved in siting key facilities." Environmentalists believed the provision would enable the federal government to force states to locate energy facilities. Calfee was waiting for the move and was able to get the provision removed. He argued that energy siting should be handled in a separate bill.

The land use bill was not powerful environmental legislation. The environmentalists who supported it did so on the assumption that it provided some leverage to fight the developers—both the powerful federal public works agencies like the Corps of Engineers and the Federal Highway Administration, and the big private developers who were, according to Calfee, "able to sell unsophisticated small communities a bill of goods about the benefits their projects would bring." Calfee's strategy was "to put special burdens on development in critical areas. In this way," he said, "you might succeed in preserving by default. At least you put the local community and the antidevelopment people in a better position to bargain."

The land use bill never attained the status of a major issue on the calendar of traditional grassroots conservation organizations. A vague bill, it promised the environmentalists few tangible gains. When it met with strong opposition in the House, the environmentalists failed to rally strong grassroots support for its defense.

THE OPPOSITION: THE CHAMBER ORCHESTRATES

From 1970 until mid-1973, opposition to the land use bill was muted and unorganized. Conservatives in Congress liked the states-rights emphasis of the bill—as a policy-neutral planning and procedural bill without sanctions and with the federal role limited to handing out money. In the beginning, the concept of state land use planning was endorsed by a fragile alliance held together by the magic word "balance." Mining, timber, grazing, and agricultural interests, the housing industry, and even the U.S. Chamber of Commerce supported the need for balanced planning by the states.

However, the Chamber was unhappy with the role assigned to the federal government by the bill. Federal bureaucrats were to review state planning procedures, a review that Jackson insisted would be limited to insuring the "good faith" efforts of states. The Chamber, on the other hand, felt that federal control was inescapable if federal review were allowed. In the beginning, Dan Denning, the Chamber's leading lobbyist on the bill, tried to eliminate the provision for federal review. When that effort failed, the Chamber decided to devote major time and resources to outright defeat of the land use bill. It was a critical decision because, as the debate took shape, Denning provided the analysis that made it possible for the bill's opponents in the Congress to carry on the fight. The explanation is largely a simple matter of timing.

By late 1972, the economic and social impact of earlier environmental legislation was beginning to be felt. Many of the earlier environmental bills, such as the Coastal Zone Management bill, had been either ignored or inactively opposed by the business community during Congressional passage. A lobbyist for the homebuilders explained that "when NEPA passed, I had a major housing bill and a major tax bill to worry about. I didn't have *time* to think about NEPA. I'd *find* the time if I had it to do over."

By 1972-73, the business community was finding the time to think about environmental legislation. In 1973, for example, the National Association of Realtors set up the position of staff director for energy and the environment in its legislative office. Other corporate and trade interests followed this example. When the land use bill came along, Denning and others saw it as another bill in the tradition of NEPA, the recent Clean Air Act, and the Water Pollution Control Act. All of these measures were being interpreted in the courts and implemented by regulations in ways unforeseen by many of the bills' supporters in Congress.

Among the many analyses of the land use bill that Denning wrote was an article called "Emerging Growth Strategies." In this article, which was widely distributed, Denning argued that the land use bill was the third part of a trinity, composed also of air pollution laws and water pollution laws. He argued that "without genuine public understanding of the issues a policy has developed that will determine much about how the United States will grow in the years ahead. . . . The effects of these three measures on growth come via not only the provisions of the actual legislation, but also through their judicial and regulatory offspring."[4]

Denning's first reaction to the bill was that "It looked like a panacea for a whole set of problems that nobody begins to understand." Like many others, he found both the ends sought and means proposed in the measure difficult to pin down. At first he objected to the bill on the ideological grounds that federal bureaucrats use new federal programs to push their own prejudices (often unintentionally). "It is naive to suppose that federal dollars will lead to anything other than an imposition of federal (and bureaucratic) policy objectives," he said. But it wasn't until the 93rd Congress that Denning had the arguments he needed to make the bill a subject of major debate.

In July 1973, CEQ had published *The Taking Issue,* which argued for expanding public control over private property. Earlier, in May 1973, the Rockefeller Task Force report, *The Use of Land,* was unveiled. The report argued that:

The protection of critical environmental and cultural areas will require placing tough new restrictions on the use of private land. These restrictions will be little more than delaying actions if the courts do not uphold them as reasonable measures to protect the public interest, in short, as restrictions that land owners may fairly be required to bear without payment by the government.

Denning declared, "All my vague fears about the bill crystallized. Those guys were proposing a massive assault on private property rights to protect nature. I had listened to the perfunctory debate in the Senate when the bill first passed and I *knew* those guys didn't understand the implications of the bill they were voting for. I decided that if we're going to make revolutionary changes in the traditional concept of property rights, we should at least have a public debate. It shouldn't slip through unnoticed in some 'motherhood environmental' bill."

---

4. Denning cited recent EPA proposed transportation plans which would reduce traffic in Los Angeles by 82 percent and a Supreme Court decision that quality in areas of relatively pure air could not be reduced—a decision with major implications for the location of new industry in rural areas.

During the 93rd Congress, Denning succeeded in reversing the position of some Senate Interior Committee members who had supported the bill in the 92nd Congress. The minority views in the Committee report on the bill, for example, repeat verbatim the arguments made against the bill in Chamber publications. But Denning believed the bill was unbeatable in the Senate.

Denning's effort to defeat the bill was nearly a full-time job for more than a year. He gathered together a number of opponents and potential opponents who met frequently in Washington to discuss the bill and worked to convince them that (1) the bill could be defeated in the House, and (2) the bill had strong antigrowth implications and would affect many economic interests in ways they failed to understand. Denning convinced the construction trade unions that the bill would affect them adversely, and they became active lobbyists against the bill. Others in Denning's shifting group included the National Association of Manufacturers, representatives of mining and timber interests, the Farm Bureau, the National Association of Homebuilders, and the National Association of Realtors.

Not all of those who met with Denning agreed with him, and some opposed the bill for other reasons. Denning was, nevertheless, responsible for raising the issues that led to the bill's defeat and for mobilizing an otherwise ambivalent and inactive opposition.

Denning wrote a number of newsletters and special analyses of the bill that were widely circulated. He portrayed the bill as an entering wedge for federal zoning and as a confiscatory measure that might deprive private property owners of use of their land without compensation. A newsletter entitled "Without Just Compensation," which the Chamber sent out in early 1974, is typical.

Suppose you own land in the country, near a major metropolitan area. You bought this land with your savings, many years ago, as an investment. . . maybe to put the kids through college, when the time comes. . . . Up to now, if the government wanted this land of yours for public purposes in say a highway interchange— it had to pay a fair price for it. What if the government declares it in the public interest to "preserve open space" and says you may continue to own your land, but you may not build anything on it?

Believe it or not, there are "experts" in Washington advocating such government policies.

The steady flood of such communications to local businessmen prompted a major letter-writing campaign to members of Congress.

In Congress, Denning worked with Steiger, a conservative opponent of new federal programs who, according to a member of the Interior Committee staff, "likes to bait the environmentalists." Steiger made the Chamber arguments both in the Committee and in discussions with other members of Congress. Steiger might have opposed this bill without the Chamber's urging, but without the Chamber's assistance he would not have been able to carry out his campaign to defeat the bill. The one minority staff man with the Committee favored the bill and worked for the Republicans who supported it.

The combination of grassroots opposition on an issue as volatile and complex as property rights, heavy lobbying among the mining, timber, farm interests and construction trades, and the Chamber, coupled with the confusion engendered by the Administration's defection, were sufficient to defeat the bill.

VII. Summary and Conclusion

The National Land Use Policy Bill was characterized by one member of the House Interior Committee as ". . . the most misunderstood piece of legislation which has emerged from the House Interior Committee during the 14 years I have served as a member. . . ." Since the bill failed to specify policy ends, the debate was shaped by widely varying interpretations of both intent and effect that could not easily be proved or disproved. The set of assumptions that underlay the bill were never explained or explored. The problems the bill was intended to address were never defined. Instead, proponents and opponents engaged in a massive rhetorical attack and counterattack based only on hopes and fears about possible outcomes.

Absent an understanding of the interplay among the social, economic and technological forces that determine the way in which growth occurs, the authors of the various bills sought explanations for patterns they found objectionable and proposed solutions that fit their needs, but neither the assessments of problems nor prescriptions for solution were supported by objective evidence. The proponents and opponents of the bill accepted or rejected the arguments offered based on their assessments of whether they would win or lose should a bill be enacted.

The bill that was debated was actually two different bills, each with a separate set of assessments and prescriptions, shaped in both cases by institutional and personal perspectives that defined the facts in different ways. The Jackson bill, both as originally introduced and as melded into the combined Jackson/Administration bill, proposed public planning as the way to allocate resources so as to ameliorate social conflict and to produce a better (though undefined) balance between environmental protection and development.

State planning was proposed as an antidote to conflicting federal programs that shape the use of land and to private development that, according to Jackson and his staff, ignores the long-term public interest. Better data and public participation were offered as the keys to resolution of conflict.

The Administration bill rested on the assumption that the evidence was in—that the public was persuaded of the need to protect natural systems and amenities, but that local land use controls were thwarting the public will. Institutional reform was the proposed solution.

SUPPORT AND OPPOSITION

The arguments over the national land use bill, though carried on in ideological terms, were more often than not based on an assessment of where the best interest of competing groups lay. State planning versus the private market was not an issue so long as various interest groups were able to believe that their particular interests might prevail. In much the same way, the level of government at which the decisions should be made rested on assessments of relative strength at each of the levels of government. Implicit in the federal zoning charge was the assumption that the federal government would respond in a way that was antithetical to the interests of those who made the charge. The environmentalists first looked to the states to protect interests that were not protected by local government but when power relationships between the development communities and the environmentalists began to swing toward the environment at least on the local level, the environmentalists began to perceive the states as captives of the business community.

In the absence of any evidence, the bill was supported by those who, like Jackson, hoped that state planning would accommodate both resource protection and development and eliminate much of the controversy surrounding land use issues. It was supported by many who shared a naive hope that "thinking about" the problems would lead to environmental protection. It was supported by some who hoped that the state plan would provide an opportunity for control over federal programs they opposed and by representatives from western states who saw state land use plans as the vehicle for coordinating federal actions on the public lands with adjacent non-federal land interests. It was also supported by some developers who hoped that state intervention would put some certainty back into a game increasingly beset by local roadblocks. Environmentalists supported the bill after strengthening the "critical areas" provisions to the point where they thought the bill offered them some new leverage in their battle against the developers. In addition, the bill was supported by those ideologically disposed to the view that public decisions are preferable to allocation by the private market.

The opposition read the same bill and interpreted it differently. The opposition assessed the bill against a background of earlier environmental initiatives and the statements of both the Rockefeller Task Force and the CEQ-sponsored study, *The Taking Issue.* The opposition believed that, regardless of the language of the bill, the authors' intent had been uncovered. Most of the opposition perceived the bill not as a balanced bill but as an environmental bill with strong antigrowth implications. The opponents were those interest groups which stood to lose in any large-scale effort to regulate private property for environmental ends. They were farmers, timber owners, grazing-land owners, and other owners of undeveloped land, as well as housing and construction interests. Also in opposition were conservatives who reject government solutions as bureaucratic solutions that bear little relationship to real need.

In the end, the debate was between the same conflicting interests the original Jackson bill was meant to accommodate. The core of the bill, and the heart of the controversy, were the provisions relating to control of critical areas. The bill's effectiveness as environmental legislation depended on the strength of those provisions and assumptions about how states would proceed to develop their programs. The opposition attack rested on fears about the effect of the provisions; the proponents' support, their hopes.

THE TAKING ISSUE

The taking issue was the most troubling issue of all. In part it rested on a misunderstanding of the historical evolution of land use controls. Controls were rejected on ideological grounds but those who opposed were simply not persuaded that the purposes were essential to the public welfare. Regulation was supported by those who thought it would be employed to further their interest in protecting the natural environment.

Supporters of the bill in both the House and the Senate sought to calm opponents' fears with amendments stating that the bill would in no way alter existing constitutional doctrine. But the opponents, convinced that eager public servants would attempt to extend their control over vast areas of privately owned land to further personal and bureaucratic ends, were not reassured. In the final days of debate Congressman John Anderson of Illinois offered several amendments accompanied by a letter that addressed the opposition's concerns. As the letter explained,

Boiler plate language such as the committee bill's disclaimer that nothing in the Act should diminish or enhance constitutionally protected property rights has little practical significance because these rights are nowhere codified, but instead reside in a shifting body of widely varying and sometimes inconsistent judicial precedents. Congress cannot directly legislate on the body of case law one way or the other.

However, adoption of either the committee bill or the substitute will necessarily mean significant new efforts to regulate land uses; actions which may test the protection currently afforded property owners by judicial interpretation of the takings clause. In particular, the newly-created state land use bureaucracies may be tempted to employ regulation powers in areas which go beyond the limits that generally prevail at present.

Safeguards are needed to restrain these bureaucratic tendencies and to force state and local land-use agencies to recognize that the achievement of some thoroughly proper land-use objectives (such as preserving scenic areas or providing more open space) will require *compensation* of landowners to be constitutionally permissible.

WOULD IT HAVE MATTERED?

Even had the bill passed, would it have made any difference? This is a question to which there are no final answers. Since it is not clear what kind of a difference the bill intended, its effects could hardly have been measured in advance. One can make some tentative judgments—that planning is not going to solve land use conflicts that are expressions of fundamental value conflicts, that institutional reform is not apt to result in the imposition of either unwanted regulation or development at the local level, and that a federal bill encouraging regulation may nudge it along, but will not be effective in the face of local opposition.

As a state planning bill, the proposal rested on the assumption that better data and public participation were the keys to resolving conflicts and bringing environmental concerns into a better balance with development needs. While better data can illuminate the trade-offs involved and thereby inform the decision process, policy ends remain a matter of social choice. A major difficulty with the land use bill was that the failure to specify policy ends or to suggest policy alternatives made it impossible to determine what information was relevant to the choices which must be made. Though the Jackson staff hoped that information about the land's carrying capacity or, as proposed in the original bill, a land classification system, would provide the key to making trade-offs, no evidence was offered that either of these concepts could provide that elusive rule for allocating land outside the private market. Public participation may be both inevitable and desirable but it is not apt to ease the task of making resource allocations unless one is willing to assume a basic agreement on goals. This is manifestly not the case where interests compete over a particular piece of land. And as the debate over the land use bill revealed, public decisions are often made by a small handful of people in positions of power.

As a proposal for institutional reform the bill is equally difficult to assess. Both the Jackson bill and the Administration bill had proposed strengthening the hand of the state for reasons that had little to do with the effectiveness of the state in coming to grips with the murky problems involved. There is little reason to assume that states would be immune to the same competing, conflicting pressures that prompted introduction of the bill in the first place or that they are better situated or equipped to resolve land use conflicts.

The real lessons of the land use debate are to be found not in an examination of the bill itself, but in an evaluation of the effectiveness of the legislative process in coming to grips with the complex set of issues involved in the growth/preservation debate. The history of the land use bill would suggest that it is wrong to expect solutions to emerge out of a process that is better suited to making compromises where fairly clear interests and ends have been articulated.

In the final analysis, it is probably not wise to search for comprehensive rules to deal with land use conflicts nor to attempt to define comprehensively what land should be preserved and what kinds of development are "needed." These must be evaluated in terms of who benefits and who pays, and the trade-offs will vary according to the specific competing claims being made. The debate over the land use bill revealed that there is no consensus about benefits or losses, and little technical or scientific basis against which such values could be weighed. Until there is some agreement on ends and how they can be compared one with another, neither planning nor institutional reform is apt to alter the status quo.